WHAT'S MISSING?

MINDBENDING *Visual Riddles* FOR YOUNG SLEUTHS!

written and designed by

TILMAN REITZLE

APPLESAUCE PRESS

Kennebunkport, Maine

13-Digit ISBN: 9781604331493
10-Digit ISBN: 1604331496

This book may be ordered by mail from the publisher. Please include $3.99 for postage and handling.

Please support your local bookseller first!

Books published by Applesauce Press and Cider Mill Press Book Publishers are available at special discounts for bulk purchases in the United States by corporations, institutions, and other organizations. For more information, please contact the publisher.

CIDER MILL PRESS BOOK PUBLISHERS

"Where good books are ready for press"

12 Port Farm Road
Kennebunkport, Maine 04046

Visit us on the Web!
www.cidermillpress.com

Text and design by Tilman Reitzle
Editor: Andra Serlin Abramson

Printed in China

1 2 3 4 5 6 7 8 9 0

First Edition

PHOTO CREDITS:

All images courtesy of Shutterstock. Individual photo credits—LADYBUG: irin_k; ROBOT: Charles Taylor; CHATTERING TEETH: photosync; DINOSAUR: Barracuda Designs; TOUCAN: Eduardo Rivero; CHAMELEON: Eric Isselée; FROG: Dirk Ercken; KITE: Payless Images; CUCKOO CLOCK: Katrina Brown; FANCY CLOCK: Kai Wong; CONSTRUCTION WORKER: Luis Louro; PENCIL: Ruslan Ivantsov; RUSSIAN DOLL: Andrey Snegirev; BOXER STAMP: Alexander Zam; BEETLE: ethylalkohol; CONGO STAMP: akva; VW BEETLE: Dave Wetzel; AIRPLANE: Harry B. Lamb; PILOT: James Klotz; GOALKEEPER: Stephen McSweeny; PIGGY BANK: ajt; UNCLE SAM BANK: Steve Cukrov; PORSCHE 356: Max Earey; ROOSTER: Christian Musat; COIN: any_keen; LANTERN: Juha Sompinmäki; DRAGON: Nicha; DALMATIAN: Dan Breckwoldt; BUTTERFLIES: velora

To get you started, here is the answer to the cover riddle:

Second row from the bottom, second bug from the right: one black dot is missing from the ladybug's shell.

· HOW TO USE THIS BOOK ·

Use your **MIGHTY MAGNIFIER** to find
the one teeny tiny difference between all the like objects
on the page. If you get stuck, the colored circles on each
page will give you a clue (and some fun facts, too).
Complete answers are found on the last page,
but please, no peeking!

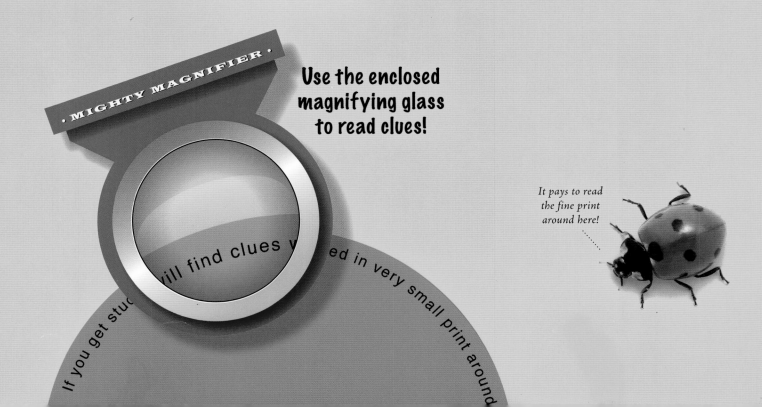

Use the enclosed magnifying glass to read clues!

It pays to read the fine print around here!

If you get stuck, will find clues ...ed in very small print around

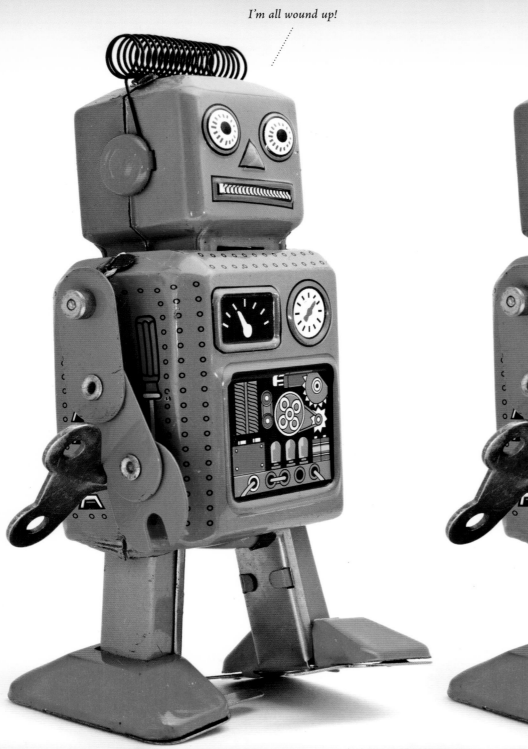

Fred

Ethel

ROBOTS

OR IS IT SOMETHING ELSE?

The word ROBOT shares its ancient Slavic roots with words such as "rabota," which means "work" in Russian.

Clue: Robbie is having a hard time keeping up. Is he running out of juice?

I can't keep up!

Robbie

Hey, keep it down!

Ralf

I'm on first!

Bud & Elvis

I'll be your mirror!

Lou & John

Ho, ho!

Ed & Johnny

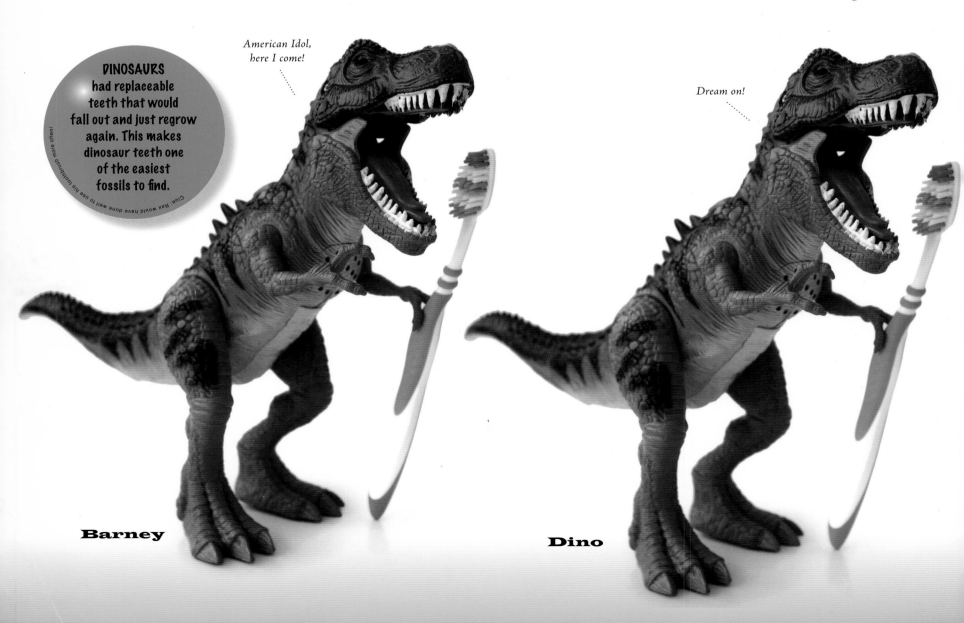

DINOSAURS had replaceable teeth that would fall out and just regrow again. This makes dinosaur teeth one of the easiest fossils to find.

Clue: Rex would have done well to use his toothbrush more often!

American Idol, here I come!

Barney

Dream on!

Dino

Smiles

You look marvelous!

Kathy & Lee

Brush & Floss

For thousands of years it was believed that "tooth worms" living in a person's mouth caused TOOTH DECAY.

Clue: Apparently Mike never, ever gets wound up.

Look, Ma, no brain!

What's a brain?

Pearly & White

This tooth brush is just a fashion accessory.

Rex

That's why your breath is so scary!

Martha

You can!

Guess how many sodas I drank last night.

Let me guess: two cans.

Sam

Fidel

Skip

José

CHAMELEONS mostly use their color-changing ability to signal to other chameleons, not to hide from predators, like that toucan above.

Despite his appearance Murphy prefers not to be called 'red neck'.

ONE CRAWLING CHAMELEON IS CURIOUSLY DIFFERENT, ...

I get my lunch on the run.

You want flies with that?

Murphy

Joe

Sherlock

Ribbit.

Ribbit?

...AS IS ONE OF FOUR FROG FRIENDS.

Bubba

Kareem

THE JUNGLE

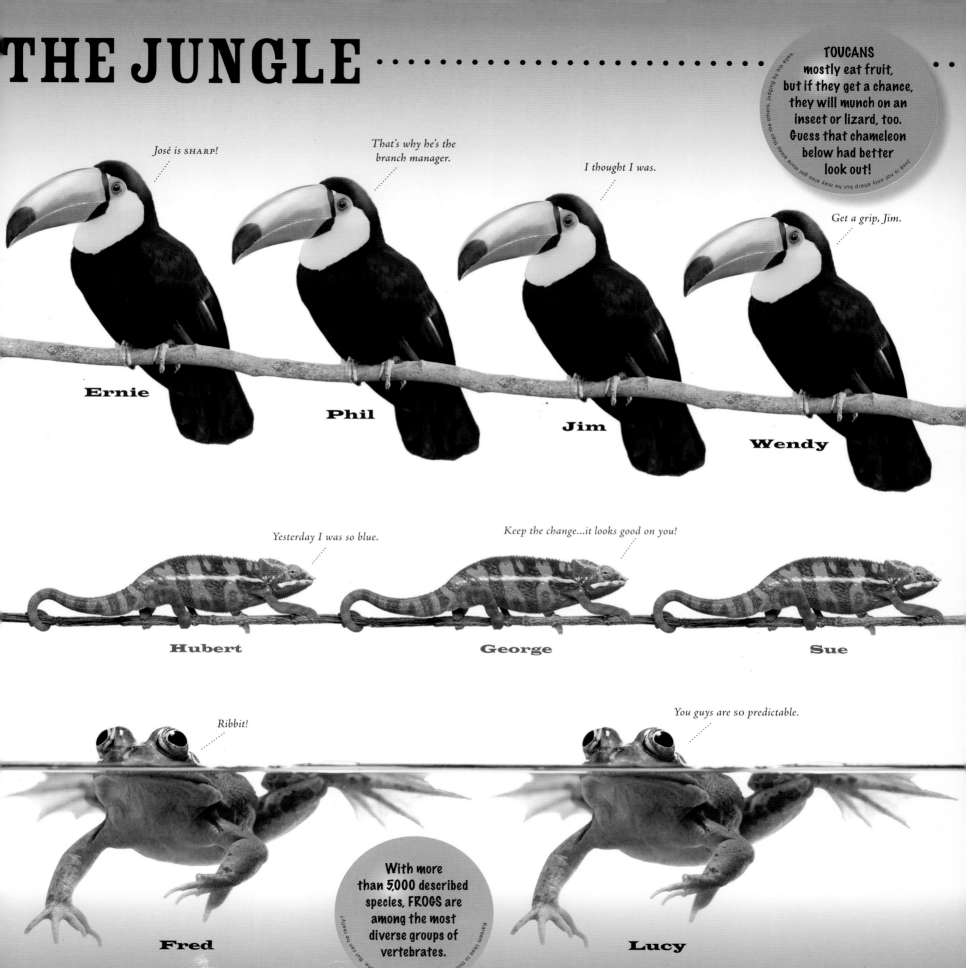

TOUCANS mostly eat fruit, but if they get a chance, they will munch on an insect or lizard, too. Guess that chameleon below had better look out!

José is not only sharp but he may also get more sleep than the others, judging by his eyes.

José is SHARP!

That's why he's the branch manager.

I thought I was.

Get a grip, Jim.

Ernie

Phil

Jim

Wendy

Yesterday I was so blue.

Keep the change...it looks good on you!

Hubert

George

Sue

Ribbit!

You guys are so predictable.

Fred

With more than 5,000 described species, FROGS are among the most diverse groups of vertebrates.

Kareem likes to think he can go toe to toe with anyone. But can he really?

Lucy

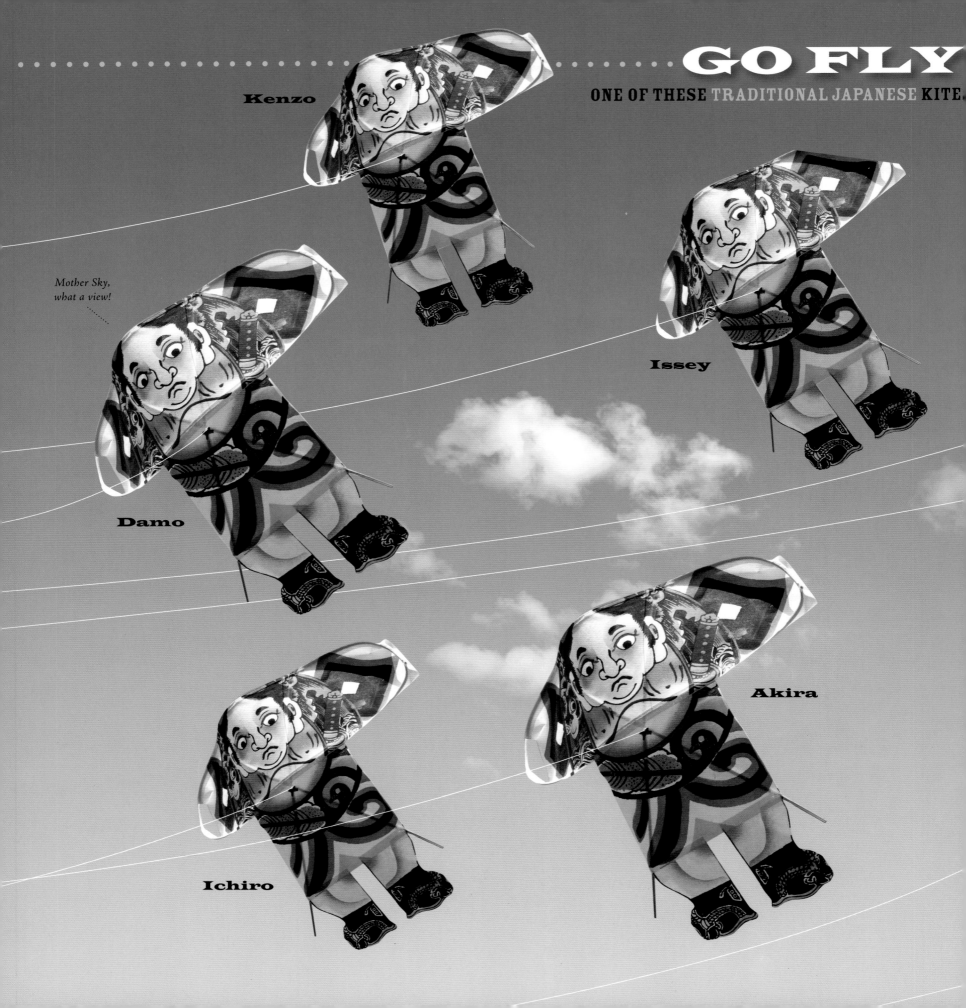

Kenzo

Issey

Damo

*Mother Sky,
what a view!*

Ichiro

Akira

The lift necessary to make a KITE fly is created when air flows over and under the kite's wing, producing low pressure above the wing and high pressure below it. This causes the kite to rise.

Clue: If you can handle it, we'll tell you that Kobe's sword is different.

Banzai! I forgot my skis.

Yukio

Ryuchi

Serious hang time!

Keiji

Kobe

IT APPEARS THAT AUNT GRETA'S CLOCKS

Cuckoo.

1)

The very first CUCKOO CLOCK is credited to the Greek mathematician, Ctesibius of Alexandria (ca.285-222 BC), who "used water to sound a whistle and make a model owl move."

Friday: Where Have All The Flowers Gone?
Cuckoo Clue: Number Four really likes Number Six.

2)

3)

Cuckoo, ALREADY?

4)

5)

ON WHICH DAY DID HER PRIZED HEIRLOOM CLOCK SEEM JUST A LITTLE OFF AND WHY?

Monday

Tuesday

Wednesday

Time

AVE GONE A LITTLE CUCKOO....

Cu-ckoo!

We're ten minutes early.

Poo-tee-weet?

6)

7)

8)

9)

10)

Thursday

Friday

Saturday

HARDLY WORKING? – – – – – – – – – – –

FORGOT SOMETHING. **WHAT DID HE FORGET AND ON WHICH DAY?**

There are many different types of CONSTRUCTION WORKERS including brick layers, carpenters, dock workers, heavy equipment operators, painters, and landscapers.

Clue: On Friday, Vito didn't bring a writing utensil.

Is that in feet or inches?

Nuts!

I'm charging overtime!

Thursday

Friday

Saturday

Nadia

*Boys!
Always fighting.*

Oksana

Irina

BOXING's first appearance in the Summer Olympic Games was in 1904 in St. Louis but the sport was not included in the 1912 games in Stockholm because Sweden's national law banned it.

Clue: Keep your eyes on the boxers feet!

You're gonna take a lickin'!   *We BOTH are!*

Alexei & Ivan

Yuri & Andrei

Boris & Mikhail

With Love ....

Don't make me come down there!

I can't watch!

Olga

Anastasia

Katerina

Oh no!

What is it?

We got cancelled!

Sergei & Ilya

Slava & Leo

Oleg & Yevgeni

Viktor & Nikolai

Sid

Boots

Hey, no cutting in.

I tried that line, too!

It's okay. I'm
with the band.

I hope this line moves soon.
I need a bathroom.

Billy

Babs

Jimmie

You are bound
to meet a lot of BEETLES
in your life since they are
the order of insects which
contains more species than
any other order in the animal
kingdom. In fact, almost
25% of all known life-
forms are beetles!

Clue: Ask Jimmie about the answer — (if you can pin him down!)

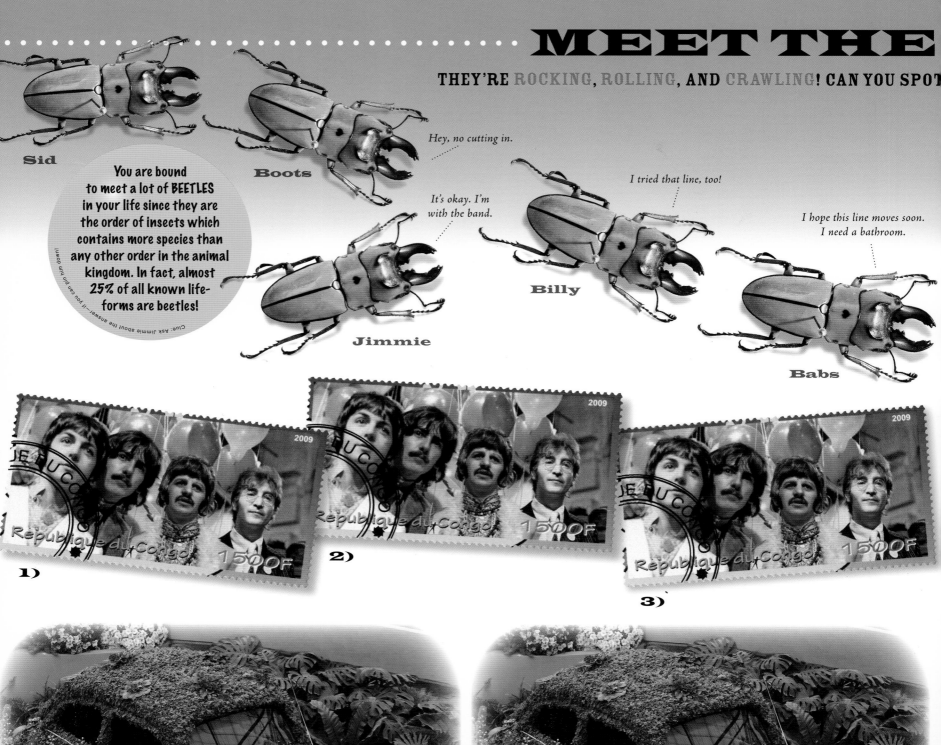

1)

2)

3)

1976

1986

BEETLES

THE ODD MEMBER IN EACH OF THESE GROUPS?

After the song "Penny Lane" became a hit for the BEATLES, the street signs for the actual Penny Lane in Liverpool disappeared so often that the town decided to just paint 'Penny Lane' on the buildings.

Cue: Have a look at the bass player's shirt.

4)

5)

6)

I've GOT to get back.

Jojo

This place is bugged!

Bugsy

I'm a traveling man... I mean BUG!

Gregor

Buddy

The VOLKSWAGEN BEETLE is the longest-running and most-manufactured automobile of a single design platform anywhere in the world.

Clue: One of these VW Beetles is missing proper rain gear.

1996

2011

Orville

Bee

The Wright Brothers were not the first to build and fly experimental AIRCRAFT, but they were the first to invent aircraft controls that made fixed-wing powered flight possible.

Clue: Herb may be wondering why his plane is so quiet today.

Snoopy

Chappie

Lindy

Manfred

Chuck

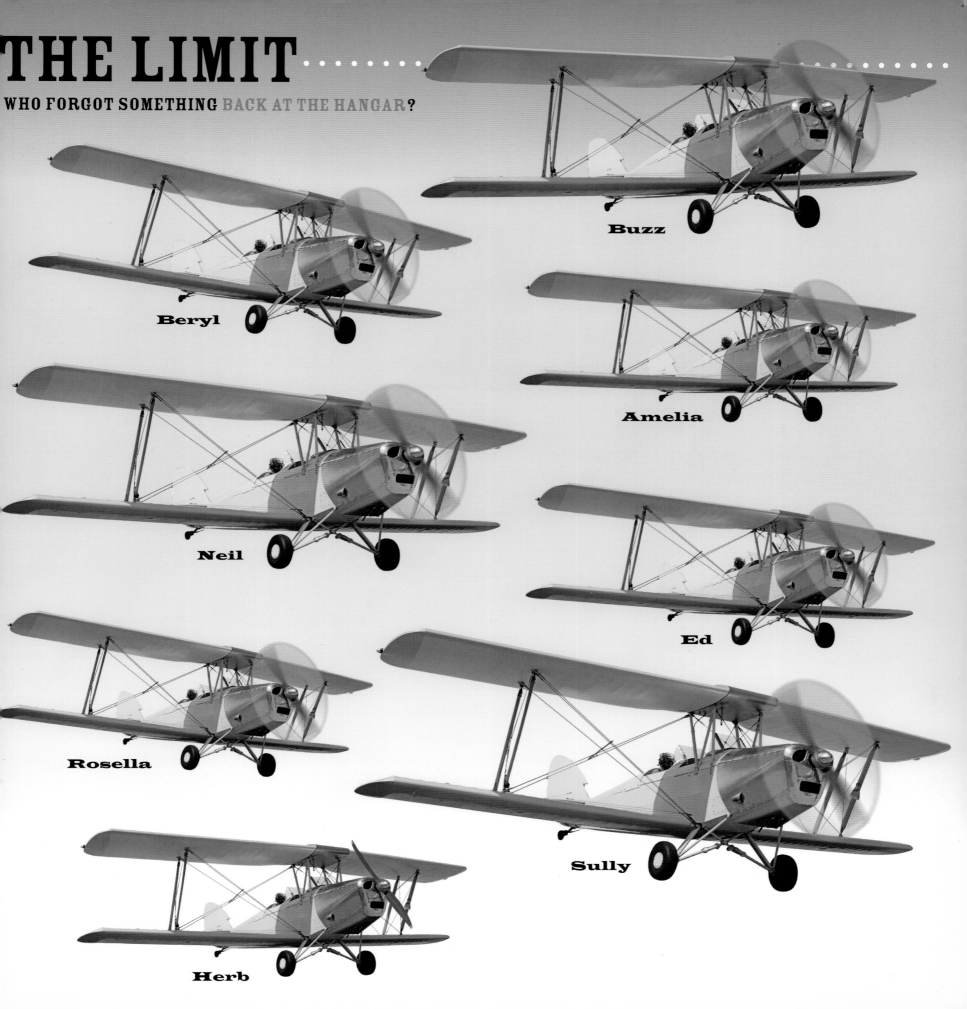

THE LIMIT
WHO FORGOT SOMETHING BACK AT THE HANGAR?

Buzz

Beryl

Amelia

Neil

Ed

Rosella

Sully

Herb

THIS GOALKEEPER IS READY FOR THE BIG TOURNAMENT

I am denying you this goal in the friendliest way possible!

Friendly Match

My goal is: No Goal!

Qualifier Game

Round of 16

The U.S.A. won the third Women's World Cup in July 1999 against the People's Republic of China. Tied for most of the game, the 5-4 win came when the Chinese goalie missed on a penalty kick.

Clue: The Final was anything but cushy for our goalie.

The only thing that's permanent is CHANGE.

Great view from up here!

Croesus

Sterling

WHICH OF THESE PIGGIES IS FINDING

A SAVE!

EVEN WITHOUT ALL OF HER GEAR. WHAT IS SHE MISSING?

Thou shalt not score!

The savings add up.

Quarterfinal

Semifinal

Final

COINS are like potato chips. You can't just have ONE!

I like a diet rich in minerals—especially copper and zinc!

While most coins are round, there have been square, guitar, sword, and Europe shaped coins. They sound like fun but we're not sure they would fit in the opening of this PIGGY BANK.

Clue: Keep an eye on Froogie's right front leg.

Nelson

Froogie

HIMSELF A LITTLE SHORT-CHANGED?

UNCLE SAM, a personification of the U.S. government originally used during the War of 1812, is shown as an elderly man with white hair and a beard, dressed in red, white, and blue clothing.

Clue: The second cousin's penny makes no sense.

ONE OF THE COIN-HUNGRY CONTRAPTIONS BELO

Penny for your thoughts.

Uncle Sam

Can I interest you in some interest-free interest?

Brother-in-law Sam

THE MONEY!

IS NOT LIKE ITS IDENTICAL PALS. CAN YOU FIND WHO'S NOT MAKING CENTS?

A penny saved is a penny earned.

Heads or Tails?

Second Cousin Sam

Uncle Ben

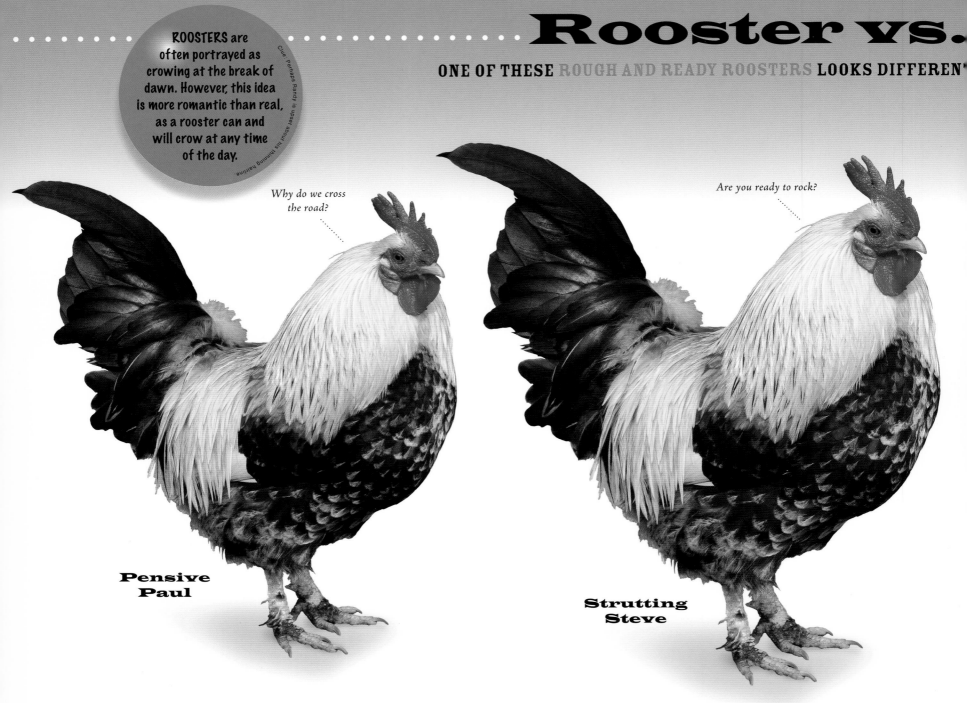

ROOSTERS are often portrayed as crowing at the break of dawn. However, this idea is more romantic than real, as a rooster can and will crow at any time of the day.

Clue: Perhaps Randy is upset about his thinning hairline

ONE OF THESE ROUGH AND READY ROOSTERS **LOOKS DIFFEREN**

Why do we cross the road?

Are you ready to rock?

Pensive Paul

Strutting Steve

THIS CAR LOOKS AS NEW **AS THE DAY IT LEFT THE SHOWROOM OVER 50 YEARS AGO...EXCEPT FOR ONE** LITTLE DETAIL. **WHAT WENT MISSING ON WHICH DAY?**

June 12   **June 13**   **June 14**

Roadster

I plan on getting the worm.

What's with the magnifying glass, big shot?

Rude Randy

Early Earl

The car below is not actually a ROADSTER. A roadster is a two-seat car, WITHOUT a fixed roof, and since the car below has a regular roof, it is just a sporty car.

Clue: On June 15, our driver had the hardest time putting air in his tire.

June 15

June 16

June 17

ONE OF THESE **LUCKY COINS** REFUSES TO BE JUST LIKE THE OTHERS

1)
2)
3)
4)
5)
6)
7)
8)
9)

RED LANTERNS ALL LOOK ALIKE?
ONE BEGS TO DIFFER....

Traditional Chinese **PAPER LANTERNS** like these are used on the fifteenth day of the Chinese New Year for the Lantern Festival.

Clues: Lantern—Find the fish! Coin—Find the dragons. Dragon—Check the fingernails.

Han

Shang

Xin

NEVER TELL A DRAGON HE OR SHE LOOKS JUST LIKE **SOMEONE** YOU KNOW!

Breath of Fire!

Let's Cha Cha!

Maude

Lee

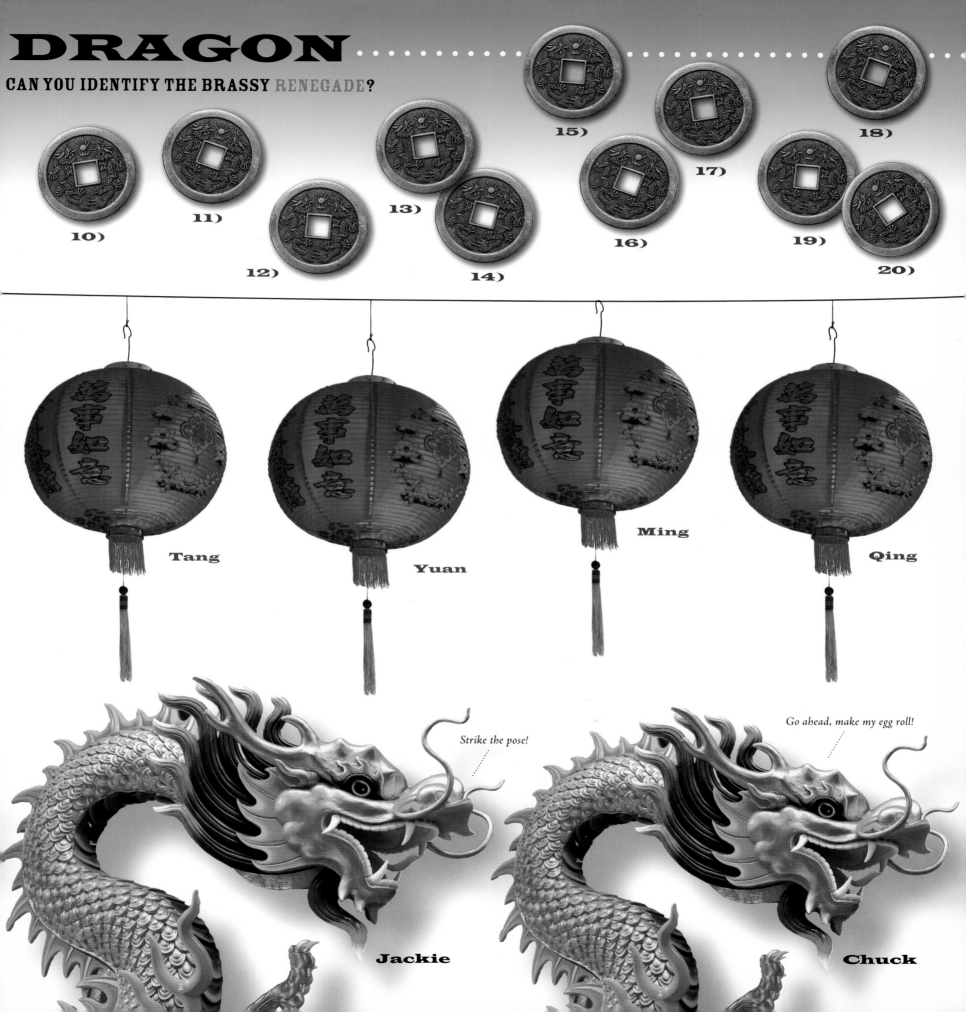

DRAGON

CAN YOU IDENTIFY THE BRASSY RENEGADE?

10)

11)

12)

13)

14)

15)

16)

17)

18)

19)

20)

Tang

Yuan

Ming

Qing

Strike the pose!

Go ahead, make my egg roll!

Jackie

Chuck

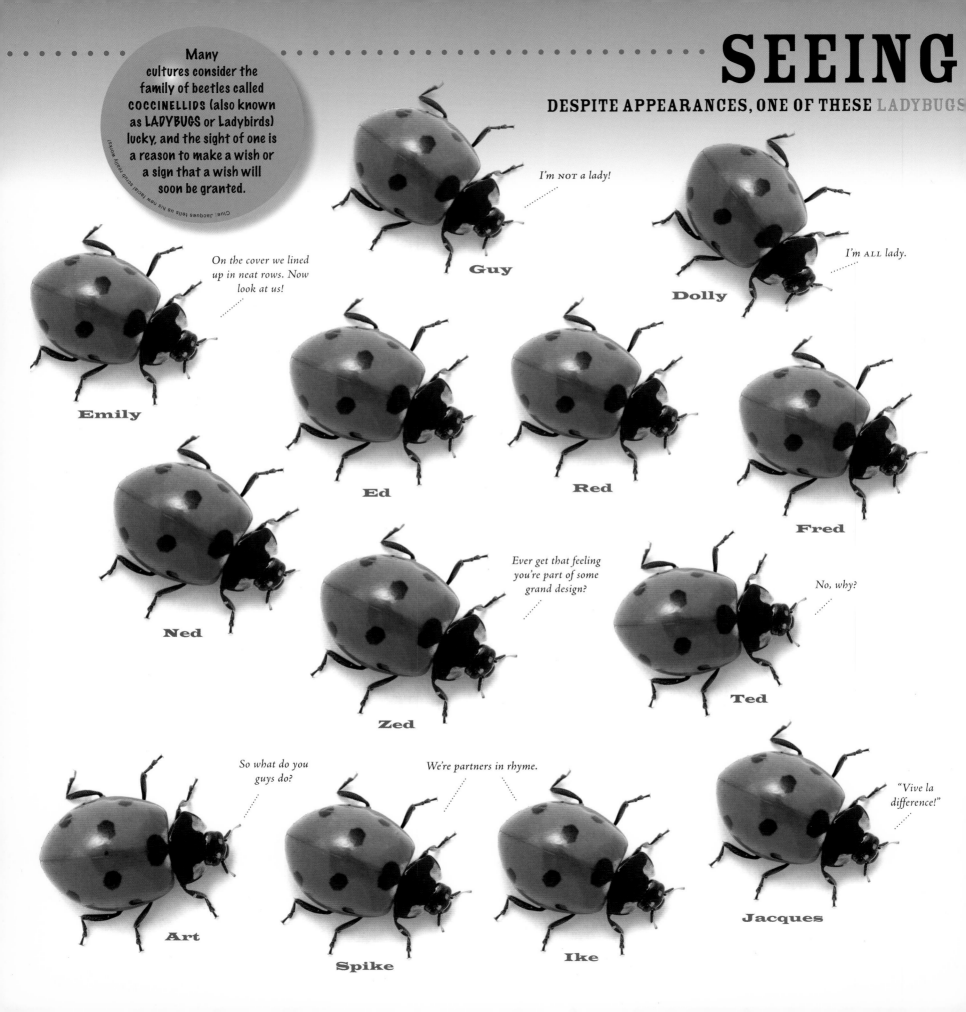

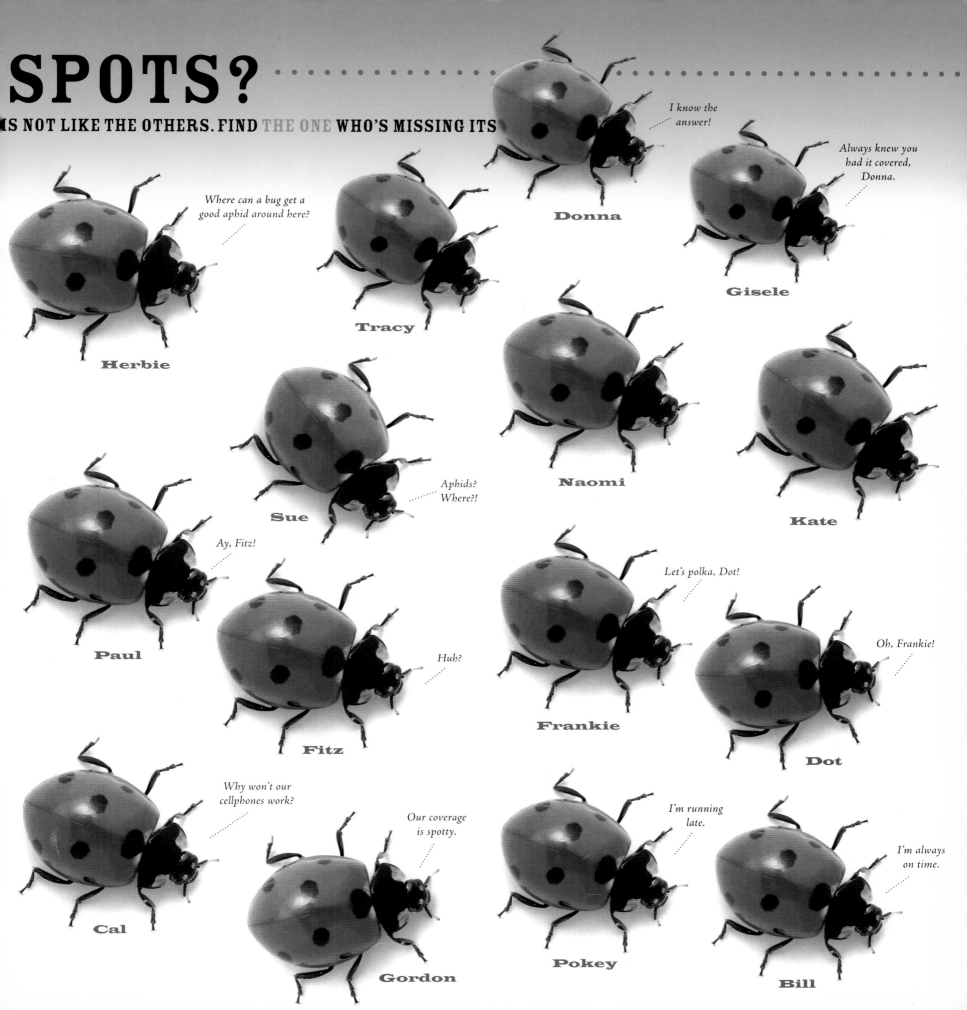

DALMATIANS were once popular with fire departments because they were known to get along well with the horses used to pull the fire engines.

Clue: Zsa Zsa appears to be very partial to those about sharing her telephone number!!

I hope there's a treat at the end of this exercise.

Dodie	Jody	Spottie	Dottie	Lotte

Meredith	Bibi	Bella	Stella	Gigi	Macy

Donna	Ella	Tipsy	Ripsie	Lucky	Trixie

Butterflies!

(YOU MAY JUST GET THEM TRYING TO FIND THE WINGED WONDER WHO'S DIFFERENT.)

Pea

Farfalle

Leo

Ina

Ace

Beatrix

Bessie

Beny

Mae

Marlene

Bruce

Elizabeth

Louise

Fela

Theo

Linda

Marilyn

Tito

Paul

Wayne

Dinah

Buddy

Victoria

Ione

Stevie

Mariposa

Greta

Marcello

Muddy

Elvis

Papillon

Denny

Bootsy

Walter

Billie

Porter

Pablo

Mary

Marlon

In autumn, some species of **BUTTERFLY** travel more than 2,500 miles in order to escape the freezing temperatures of winter.

Clue: Keep your eye on the Monarch butterfly named after a Dutch queen.

Ava

Give up yet? Of course not!

But if you want to see if you were correct, train your
MIGHTY MAGNIFIER on the answers below:

We Are the Robots

Robbie is missing one of the red and yellow batteries.

Million Dollar Smile

Kathy is missing the white wind up button near her molars.
Rex is missing a molar.

Bungle In The Jungle

José is missing the blue circle around his eye.
Murphy is missing a green spot above his shoulder.
Kareem is missing a toe.

Go Fly a Kite!

The handle of Kobe's sword is missing the lower gold rivet.

Funny Time

Cuckoo Clock #4 is missing an "I" from the Roman numeral 7 (VII)—it's only a 6.
On Friday, a leaf ornament is missing just below the clock face on the left.

Working Hard…

On Friday, Vito is missing the pencil from his tool belt.

From Russia With Love

Nadia's bow is missing the pink flower bud on the left.
Ilya's left shoe is missing the stripes.

Meet the Beetles

Beetle Jimmie is missing the pin in his back.
On stamp #4, Paul (the Beetle on the left) is missing a button on his jacket.
The 2011 Beetle is missing a windshield wiper.

The Sky's the Limit

Herb missed starting his engine altogether!

What a Save!

During the Final, the goalie's sweater is missing the
round nobbies from the right elbow pad.
Froogie is missing the top coin near his right front leg.

Show Me the Money!

The Second Cousin's penny is missing the word "cent".

Rooster vs. Roadster

Rude Randy's comb—his head ornamentation—is missing a "tooth."
On June 15, the front left wheel is missing the air valve.

Enter the Dragon

On the thirteenth coin, the left dragon is missing its right talon.
The lantern named "Ming" is missing the left fish ornament.
Dragon "Jackie" is missing the small claw on his talon.

Seeing Spots

Jacques is missing two white spots on the front of his head.

Thirty-Five Dalmatians

Zsa Zsa is missing the telephone number on her tag.

Butterflies!

Beatrix, a monarch butterfly, is missing an
orange spot in the corner on each upper wing.

About Applesauce Press

APPLESAUCE PRESS was created to press out the best children's books found anywhere. Like our parent company, Cider Mill Press Book Publishers, we strive to bring fine reading, information, and entertainment to kids of all ages. Between the covers of our creatively crafted books, you'll find beautiful designs, creative formats, and most of all, kid-friendly information on pressing [important] topics. Our Cider Mill bears fruit twice a year, publishing a new crop of titles each spring and fall.

"WHERE GOOD BOOKS ARE READY FOR PRESS"

Visit us on the Web at www.cidermillpress.com or write to us at: 12 Port Farm Road, Kennebunkport, Maine 04046